# SHIFTING *to* THE *Positive*

## A WOMAN'S GUIDE TO POSITIVE THINKING

# NINA MADSEN

*Special Art Development*

*Shifting to the Positive*

A Woman's Guide to Positive Thinking

*Nina Madsen*

Paperback ISBN: 979-12-5553-004-6
support@specialartbooks.com
www.specialartbooks.com

© Copyright 2023 — Nina Madsen, Special Art

# Table of Contents

# Introduction

Life has its ups and downs, and sometimes it can feel like we're riding on a rollercoaster all on our own. The ups are wonderful, they make us feel good and remind us why we're here, but then the downs can dash those happy thoughts. The down times make us feel insecure and uncertain. We start to wonder if we know where we're going. Are we headed down the right path? Do we know who we are as a person?

But the thing about life is that it will always have ups and downs, but your feelings about life and your feelings about yourself do not have to follow that pattern of ups and downs. You can stay strong and enjoy all that life has to offer. You can also enjoy all that you have to give to the world even through those down times.

But how? Getting to that stage in life where you can appreciate even weathering the storm can happen through positive thinking. I know the term 'positive thinking' can be a bit vague. The term often makes it seem like it's so easy or that it'll instantly change

everything if you just think about good things. But don't stop reading just yet.

That's not the case. Positive thinking, while it is about thinking positively, is also about changing your life to focus more wholly on the positive. Instead of facing squarely towards the darkness and the stress of hard times, face forward to the joys of the good times!

Not only will it help you get out of those rough times, but it will also give you greater confidence, love, and appreciation for yourself. Now, that's something to celebrate.

In these pages, you'll learn how to change your outlook through changing your career trajectory. You'll discover how to celebrate your strength by embracing alone time, and to recharge your energy by nourishing yourself. And you'll also uncover the secret of how to love your perseverance and love yourself, through sparking your creativity and showing yourself some gratitude.

Positive thinking and a positive outlook on life are inside this book, right at your fingertips. But it all starts with you. Loving yourself will help you look at the world and your life in a whole new way.

# Part One: Change Your Outlook

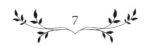

# Chapter One

## Change Your Career Trajectory

> " Give light and people will find the way.
> —*Ella Baker* "

Having a fulfilling career and a job that you love is a gift that everyone should have. You may be reading this right now while enjoying your break time at work, or maybe you're winding down after a stressful day of doing the same thing over and again. You can spend thousands of hours cultivating a career, but is it really the career that you want? One of the big obstacles to positive thinking is being in a career path that's headed nowhere or at least not in the direction you want.

Work stress can take over your thinking and really drown out all the other positive things in your life. While a career shouldn't be everything, it is part of our bigger picture. It's the way we make money and hopefully, it's a chance for you to challenge yourself and grow as an individual.

Whatever the reason for your current career path, if you find yourself struggling to think about the positives in the future, it may be time for a change.

## PUT IT INTO PRACTICE

Take some time to reflect on your current career. I'm using the word career to classify any type of job. From a lawyer to a waitress, each career takes its own shape. If it's a job that gives you the bulk of your income, then it goes under the career category.

Start asking yourself some questions about your career, such as:

- How is my job benefitting me? Maybe it's a place to create, a safe place to learn new things, or has great access to resources.

  ..................................................................................

  ..................................................................................

- If I don't love my job, are there still ways it could benefit me?

  ..................................................................................

  ..................................................................................

- Has my career negatively affected me? How?

  ..................................................................................

  ..................................................................................

- Do I need a whole change of career to help my happiness and positive outlook on life?

  .................................................................................

  .................................................................................

- What options are out there for me?

  .................................................................................

  .................................................................................

- What are my overall goals with this job?

  .................................................................................

  .................................................................................

## CREATIVE EXERCISE

Design (or find) a symbol that represents your career field. This could be anything from a chef's hat to a briefcase. Think of it as a symbol of power and strength, helping you reach your goals.

As you're designing, think of changes you want to make to your symbol as your career trajectory shifts. Maybe the chef's hat turns into a police cap, for example. Or a waitress' apron turns into a bank teller's name tag.

Whatever you choose, that image is an image of power in the field that you designed. The stronger you feel in your job of choice, the more positively you'll look at life.

## Conclusion

Sometimes, we can get so down about our jobs that we just want to get out. Take some time to look inward. Maybe there are positive things within your career that can help encourage you to keep going.

Those positive qualities can even help you chase your dreams and goals!

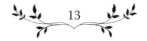

# Chapter Two

## Be Your Own DJ

> **"** Music acts like a magic key, to which the most tightly closed hearts open.
> —*Maria von Trapp* **"**

Music of all genres has power. Hearing your favorite song can make your day go from bad to amazing in the space of a few seconds. Listening to music, especially music we love, can help us get out of our own heads and just learn to enjoy the present moment. This whole book is about turning towards the light and the positive, and music can help you do that.

The right melody can help you relax, let go of your stress, and get into a dance or sing out loud. For this exercise, I want you to be your own DJ.

Make music more of a focus in your life, and let it act as a refuge for you when you're going through one of those tough times.

## Put It into Practice

Take a little time to think about what songs are your favorites. Make a list and write it down in your journal. Note why each of these songs is important to you, and how it connected to that time of your life.

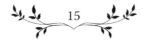

How did it make you feel? Did it help you get through some difficult times? Did it encourage and inspire you? Why?

.................................................................................................................

.................................................................................................................

.................................................................................................................

.................................................................................................................

Then, start to play music every day, whether it's your favorite songs or a mixture of random new songs. Introduce music more into your life whenever you need a jolt. Play it while you and your family are making dinner, in the morning, or while you're taking a bath.

Think of music as an escape and a safe place. A guide to help you start seeing the brighter things in life.

## CREATIVE EXERCISE

Create an awesome playlist of your favorite songs! Use your favorite app to compile and organize your songs. Put them in an order that feels right to you.

I encourage you to create multiple playlists to fit certain moods or situations. You could have a playlist for use after a hard day at work, a playlist to relax, and a playlist for working out.

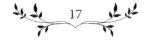

# Conclusion

Music can soothe any soul, and since life is so chaotic, why not use it to soothe yours? Make it a part of your life; use it to your own advantage, and let it help you to keep looking up.

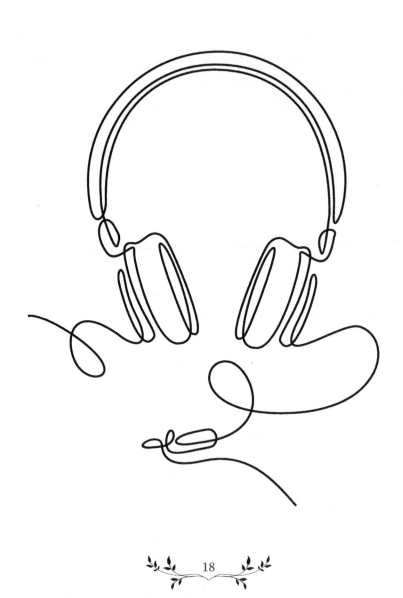

# Chapter Three

## Rethink Your Role Model

> ❝
> A girl should be two things: who she wants and what she wants.
>
> —*Coco Chanel*
> ❞

We are what we idolize. Who we look up to reveals a lot about us, and sometimes, without even knowing it, we might put the spotlight on the wrong individual. All of that outward focus can quickly disconnect us from our own power and make us forget to honor ourselves.

In order to keep a positive outlook on life, it's helpful to examine what we truly care about and who we admire. As you work on changing your outlook, it's good to question yourself and what you believe in.

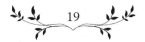

Time to delve into the ideas surrounding your role model and take a deeper look.

## Put It into Practice

Figure out who you consider to be a role model in your life. It might be several people, but let's just start with one to make it easy. As you think about this person, ask yourself:

- What is it about them that I admire?

.................................................................................

.................................................................................

- When did I start considering them a role model?

  ...................................................................................................................

  ...................................................................................................................

- What have they shown me in their actions/ words?

  ...................................................................................................................

  ...................................................................................................................

Write down seven characteristics and qualities that you admire. This could be their confidence, their charisma, or their natural grace.

Once you've got these characteristics down, start thinking about which traits you share with this person. Or perhaps which traits you'd really like to start working on because of this person. Keep in mind that you're not trying to copy this person, but rather find a connection back to your best self.

Next to each quality, write down two actions you can take which will help you progress in acquiring that quality.

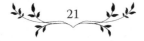

The actions could include something out of your comfort zone like volunteering, performing, or socializing more. When you're finished, you'll have a full list of what you hope to be as well as how you can get there! Now that's positive thinking.

Note: After you reflect on your role model, you might discover that they're not really a role model at all. That's ok, and that doesn't mean you're bad or wrong. But you might think about letting go of them and finding someone else whose qualities are truly admirable.

## CREATIVE EXERCISE

Draw or find a portrait of the person you admire. In your drawing, include images or list down qualities and characteristics you admire and wish to imitate.

# Conclusion

Role models help give you a focus and direction in your life. They can help you understand yourself in a new way when you admire someone, because it shows you what characteristics you can develop. Now, you have a direct path on how to get there. Cheers to progress and growth!

# Chapter Four

## Revisit a Negative Memory

> Everyone has a story to tell. Everyone is a writer, some are written in books and some are confined to hearts.
>
> —*Savi Sharma*

Unfortunately, there are so many obstacles to our happiness. Our mind's ability to stay focused on the good things in life gets challenged left and right. One of those obstacles is negative memories that we just keep holding onto.

You are not alone. We all struggle to let go of the worst moments from our past. Maybe someone wronged us and we've never really forgiven them. Or

we experienced something humiliating that left us scarred. Some of us have hurt someone else, and we can't forgive ourselves.

Whatever this negative memory is, it has power over you. Trapping negativity inside ourselves instead of letting it go poisons us with bad energy and pushes us into a dark state when we need the light.

In order to start changing your outlook, it's time to take a step, be bold, and revisit a negative memory.

## PUT IT INTO PRACTICE

Write down a memory that you've been holding onto for a long time. If you have a lot of trauma from the past, it might be easier to start with something small. Once you've found a negative image digging into your subconscious, write down every detail. Leave nothing out.

Writing can be very cathartic, helping you release bad energy. But to get the most out of it, ask yourself these questions as you work through writing your memory down.

- What else was happening in your life at this time?

  ..................................................................................

  ..................................................................................

- How did this make you feel at the time?

  ..................................................................................

  ..................................................................................

- What did you learn after all of this was over?

  ..................................................................................

  ..................................................................................

- Did this moment in your life lead to any major changes (they can be internal or external)?

  ..................................................................................

  ..................................................................................

- Imagine someone else saw this happen. Can you imagine this happening from another person's point of view? How might that look, and what might their perspective on the situation be?

.................................................................................................

.................................................................................................

Once you have the answers to these questions, take a moment to envision this memory or situation in a new way. Rewrite the story from a new perspective. Observe how you feel about it once you're done. Can you find even more valuable lessons from this memory?

## CREATIVE EXERCISE

On a separate piece of paper, draw an image that represents this retold memory and the positive lessons you learned from experiencing what you did. Hang this up somewhere where you can see it often. It can help undo the negative hold this bad memory has in your life and remind you that perspective changes everything.

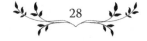

# Conclusion

Our outlook on life can be affected by the negative experiences in our lives, especially if we do not work through them and eventually let them go. In order to work on your outlook, revisit a bad memory, and see if you can't see it in a new way.

Maybe you might even ask someone outside of the memory to help you. This could be a counselor, a friend, or a family member. Get their perspective on it, if you need just a little jumpstart into turning a bad memory into one where you learned helpful lessons.

# Part Two: Celebrate Your Strength

# Chapter Five

Love Your Alone Time

> **"**
> Kindness is always fashionable,
> and always welcome.
> —*Amelia Barr*
> **"**

Part of positive thinking is taking the time to celebrate your gifts. It's important for you to take joy in your strengths and who you are as a person. As women, we often get told that we are too selfish if we want to spend time alone or that we only care about ourselves if we want to take some time out of the day to do something that's just for us.

I want to break down that lie and provide you with a new truth: loving yourself is about taking care of

yourself. You can take care of yourself as well as celebrate who you are and what you have to give by carving out alone time. When you show yourself love, you have more to give to the world.

Trust me, you'll always find an excuse as to why you can't take a day for yourself. There's work, the house, the kids... the list is endless. That's why you have to schedule some alone time for yourself and stand by it come what may. It's incredibly healthy to spend time alone. It reduces stress, helps quiet the noise in your head, and rejuvenates you like nothing else.

What you need to do is focus on what you do that's just for you and how that brings you joy.

## PUT IT INTO PRACTICE

It's so important to have a positive outlook on life when you are kind to yourself. Unfortunately, it's all too easy to forget about what everyone else needs and focus on you and your pleasure. To inspire yourself to take a day off, make a list of all the things you do in your life that are just for you.

Maybe you like to read in the morning, or maybe once a month you go and get your nails done. Perhaps there's a hiking trail you want to try by yourself or a cafe you want to sit in for a few hours. If you can't think of anything at the moment, take a deep breath and relax.

Write a reminder to yourself that you want to start focusing on activities geared towards you and no one else. You deserve to make space for yourself just as you make space for others in your life.

Once you've got your list down, see if you can add five more things to it. Make sure they are activities you want to do, not an errand or something you pick for your kids or a friend. This is a chance to revel in your interests. It can be yoga, journaling, meditation, etc. Now, put down a date in which you will do one of the activities on your list. Just you and yourself, having alone time, celebrating who you are and your strengths.

## CREATIVE EXERCISE

Draw an image of you doing something that's just for you. I want to challenge you to do a bad drawing. Rather than draw yourself perfectly, sketch a messy version of you doing something you love. This is an image of power; the power of loving yourself and giving yourself the space that you deserve.

## Conclusion

Love yourself and celebrate who you are through alone time. There is no better way to say 'I love you' to yourself than to spend some time on your own doing something you enjoy. Being alone also brings you confidence, rest, and strength.

# Chapter Six

## Advocate for Yourself

> ❝
> Step into the new story you are
> willing to create.
> —*Oprah Winfrey*
> ❞

Today is the day you start advocating for yourself, your wants, and your needs. So many women tend to gravitate toward the sidelines of life when we need to be standing front and center. It's easier to stay out of difficult situations instead of fighting because then no one is looking at us, judging us, or fighting back.

As a result, we let things slide that definitely aren't okay. You might ignore an insult to someone you love or yourself. Maybe someone's made an assertion that you just can't get behind. Or perhaps someone is

trying to take advantage of you, and it's time to fight back.

Advocate for yourself. Everyone deserves to feel safe, happy, and loved. Why let people walk all over us when we can take the strength we have from within and create boundaries? Those lines in the sand are a way to show people this is what you will and will not tolerate.

When you stop being afraid to stand up for yourself and say what you need, you show strength, courage, and love to yourself. Do not be afraid to advocate for yourself when the time is right.

## PUT IT INTO PRACTICE

Make a list of things, words, or actions people do that make you uncomfortable. Did a friend make an off-color joke that offended you? Did your boss try to make you feel small? Did your partner take advantage of you? Write down all the things that made you feel like someone's crossed a line.

When you're finished, look it over and decide which things make you the angriest and the most uncomfortable. Start to think about what you could do to set a boundary in your life and therefore avoid letting this happen again. Or, reflect on how you can let the person know you're not comfortable. Remember, this isn't about getting a specific reaction; we can't control others' words.

Instead, focus on what you can say and do to let yourself be heard. The truth is, other people tend not to like boundaries. Just be prepared for the first time you set a boundary, people may have strong reactions. That's why a lot of people prefer not to create boundaries; they don't want to create any kind of confrontation.

But setting and maintaining a boundary can also create a beautiful freedom. No longer do you have to feel trapped by other people. You can do what makes you happy and what makes you feel comfortable. Whatever happens as a result of your boundary, remember this: the important thing is that you stood your ground, and you stated your truth.

You did what was right for you and what was best for you. This is the best way to build up your confidence and belief in yourself.

## CREATIVE EXERCISE

Find a picture of you and your friends sitting together. (Or rather a picture of you in a place you felt entirely comfortable and safe to be who you needed to be.) When we know we are loved, no matter the situation, we can do what we need to do in terms of setting and sticking to our boundaries.

When you have this picture in front of you, write down how you felt when you were in that situation or with that group. What about that situation or those friends made you feel secure and connected? Attach the picture to the page so that you can always look at it when you look at the positive feelings you experienced during that moment. Try to embody those feelings as you go through your daily life. Building boundaries will get easier and easier.

# Conclusion

If you won't speak up for yourself, who else will! While connecting with others and supporting each other is important, you also need to know the strength you have inside of yourself. You can speak up for yourself and protect yourself through advocating and setting boundaries. The more you see your strengths, the more other people will begin to see them as well.

# Chapter Seven

*Rediscover Your Town*

> " Dreams and reality are opposites.
> Action synthesizes them.
> —*Assata Shakur* "

A lot of people tend to stay in the same place for years and years. It's comforting to live in a place we know inside and out, but you can get a little bored seeing the same things every day. Why not practice looking at your town through new eyes?

This practice will push you to try new things, meet new people, and enjoy your town in a way you never have before. But it will also help you to focus on the positive aspects of the place where you live and help shake you out of your rut. When we need to change

our outlook on life, it's important we challenge ourselves and keep growing even if we can't leave town.

## Put It into Practice

Get some friends together who are from your town (or look online) and compile a list of five places in your area that you've never seen or visited before. These could be restaurants, parks, activity centers, etc. The only criterion is that it has to feel new to you.

Challenge yourself to try one of these new places or activities in your town. Go into it with the perspective of being an outsider. Ask yourself these questions:

- What does your town look like to someone who's never been there before?

..................................................................................................

..................................................................................................

- What's the most exciting, the most beautiful, the most special part or place?

..................................................................................................

..................................................................................................

- What are some positive things about the town an outsider might notice?

........................................................................................

........................................................................................

## CREATIVE EXERCISE

To keep the practice of new perspectives in mind, compose a short travel article about your town. Write it in a way that will make people want to come visit. If you prefer to draw or take photos, imagine you're creating a postcard about this new experience. Think of how you might convince someone to visit the same spot. Spending time in this new perspective can really help you get out of a funk and start appreciating where you live so much more.

# Conclusion

We are very much influenced by our external world. Where you live plays a big role in how you feel about life. If you've started to grow tired of your town and what's in it, looking at it in a new way can make it feel like a whole new place.

# Chapter Eight

## Find (and Love) Your Flaws

> **"** Be messy and complicated and
> afraid and show up anyways.
> —*Glennon Doyle* **"**

This is a universal truth: we are all flawed. It doesn't have to be unfortunate, it's just a fact of life. Your flaws make you human and connect you to everyone else. It's time to stop feeling guilty about those flaws and see if you can't find something to appreciate about them.

Better yet, let's find a way to work with them. Your self image should always work to your advantage. They'll just be a natural part of you and deserve to

be celebrated. Your body is not your enemy, but a negative attitude about your looks can be a huge step backward.

So, how can you change the way you see those supposedly less-than-gorgeous parts of yourself? It starts with a self-examination.

## PUT IT INTO PRACTICE

Even though this might be a little bit tough, think about something you don't always like about yourself. Dig a little deeper than you hate how much you love chocolate. Things you might not like about yourself could include something like you always shy away from the spotlight, and you chastise yourself for it. Or you let people take advantage of you because you're a people pleaser. Or you don't have as much patience as you would like to have in stressful situations.

Now, start looking at these traits from a new perspective.

- If you're not in the spotlight, who is? Why do you think that is? Are you ready to take up some space, or are you happy to let other people shine? (Is this a true flaw or just a personality trait?)

........................................................

........................................................

- If you tend to be a people-pleaser, think about why that is. What do you get out of doing that for others? The drive to make people happy and be kind can be very positive traits. Perhaps you might consider putting this skill to good use in another field. This could be something like volunteer work or community outreach.

........................................................

........................................................

- If you're too impatient, think about the situations where you feel like you're losing your patience. What is actually going on around you? Who are the people involved, and what is causing the stress? How can you help yourself take a break the next time you feel the impatience growing?

........................................................

........................................................

List things out about yourself that you find negative. While not everything may actually turn out to be a positive trait, the majority of them will likely work in your favor. You can also brainstorm ways to turn any negative or difficult traits into positive ones by thinking about how you might work with them. How can you focus on your strengths in order to help yourself and to reframe your 'weaknesses'? Write down a few ideas of how you can turn things around and start to see what you thought was a flaw into a part of your gorgeous, internal tapestry.

## CREATIVE EXERCISE

Draw a portrait of your face (or take a picture). If you're drawing, be sure to include everything, even the things you might consider flaws such as scars. Around your face, write down the new strengths you've found inside yourself.

# Conclusion

This is you, with all your blemishes and scars both inside and out, but there is beauty too. There is light and strength, and if we turn our minds toward the positive, we can see our strengths even more clearly.

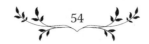

# Part Three: Love Your Energy

# Chapter Nine

## Nourish Yourself

> **"**
> This is my invariable advice to people:
> Learn how to cook–try new recipes,
> learn from your mistakes, be fearless,
> and above all, have fun.
>
> —*Julia Child*
> **"**

Your body is your vehicle and it needs your help. Taking good care of your physical body can help your other bodies (emotional, mental, spiritual) thrive. It's also a way to show yourself that you love yourself enough to take care of your body.

What we put in our bodies has an incredible effect on how we feel. This is not a diet book by any

means, but I do want you to start thinking about how you can nourish yourself. I want you to nourish your body so that your heart and mind have the best advantage possible.

Loving yourself is making sacrifices and doing what's best.

## PUT IT INTO PRACTICE

Create a list of healthy habits and foods that you already know you should be doing or consuming. Then, go through this list and check off what you already do or consume, and put a circle around those healthy things that you need to work on.

Maybe you need to start cutting out some sugar or start exercising a bit more. Perhaps you need to add a few more vegetables into your meals. Look at the list of circled items and decide which options can point you toward a healthier life.

Then, create a meal plan. Start small. For example, you can add vegetables to one meal a day. Take the same approach with exercise; start with a fifteen-minute workout then add to it week by week. If you never workout, think about how you can do something easy to help yourself move.

Now, write down a list of foods that often tempt you. Normally, these foods will not be healthy for you so it's important to see where in your life you can make some changes. There is no need to cut them out entirely, but you can cut back on anything that doesn't serve you. When you create your meal plans, you can budget for some of these extra foods that act as a treat.

## CREATIVE EXERCISE

Go to your local farmer's market and purchase a bunch of bright, colorful, fresh fruits and vegetables you might not normally buy. At home, draw them, and see yourself enjoying the beauty of healthy food.

Then, start getting creative with recipes that are both healthy and delicious. You can get inspiration anywhere online, in family cookbooks, or at the library.

# Conclusion

Taking care of yourself is about going that extra mile and doing what your body needs. The more you nourish your body, the better your mind and heart will be as well. It can be a tough road, but you won't regret it.

# Chapter Ten

## Revisit Your Junk

> **"** Keeping busy and making optimism a
> way of life can restore your faith in yourself.
> —*Eleanor Roosevelt* **"**

Who says you need a spa day to feel fresh and revitalized? Going through your things and getting rid of what you no longer wear or need can be just as refreshing. The occasional reorganization can give your life a makeover, and we all need to do it every so often.

We tend to acquire a lot of stuff. And sometimes, we hold onto stuff for no other reason than it feels good to have it around. We think, what if I need this one day? Or this is so beautiful I just can't get rid of it. But

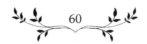

what good is stuff if it's not actually serving you or providing you with any benefit?

When we surround ourselves with so much junk that never gets used that it can become a physical representation of how we live our lives. We hold onto the things we don't really need and we stagnate. But when we refresh our possessions, we let go of useless things weighing us down. And we provide new space in our lives for more important, beneficial things.

## Put It into Practice

Let's start with clothing. That's really the easiest place to begin. Head to your closet and your chest of drawers and pull everything out. Go through it piece by piece. What do you actually wear? What do you need, and what do you love? If you haven't worn something for the past few months, (and it's not a weather-related item), then it's time for it to go. Or if it doesn't fit anymore, put it in the donate pile.

To make it easier on yourself, you can categorize your clothing into three piles. One is the love and keep pile, another is the maybe pile, and the last one is the giveaway pile. After you organize everything, go back

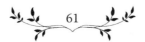

through your maybe pile again. Either put the item in the keep category or the donate bundle. That maybe pile should be completely empty.

Now, you've got a whole set of clothes that you do not need in your life anymore. Take it to a secondhand store or shelter and donate it. The clothing you chose to keep is what you truly love and now you get to enjoy it even more.

Go through the rest of your possessions in this way, and you'll be amazed at how refreshed you feel!

## CREATIVE EXERCISE

Create a closet you love! Even though we might like to keep a lot of things, no one really loves clutter. Draw a closet that you want to aspire to. It's only filled with things you want to wear all perfectly organized so that you can get to everything.

# Conclusion

It's spring cleaning time. Challenge yourself to do this purge once a year to reevaluate why you purchased something and brought it into your home. It's ok to give things away. Sometimes, being more mindful about what possessions we actually have can teach us a little bit more about ourselves and how we operate, and what we value.

But if you're able to let go of some things that no longer serve you, you can let go of the clutter and feel truly fabulous.

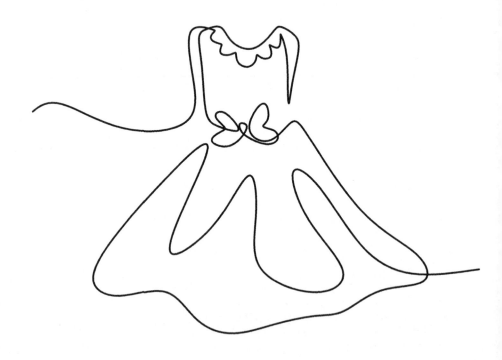

# Chapter Eleven

## Support Yourself

> " I am always busy, which is perhaps the
> chief reason why I am always well.
> —*Elizabeth Cady Stanton* "

We can't avoid work, it's a part of life. But women often overwork themselves to the point of burnout. While we all want to do well at work, it's essential that we give ourselves space to rest.

This whole book is about taking care of ourselves so that we can look at life through a positive lens. When we're realistic about how much time and energy we can spend on each task, we can take the time to care for ourselves and keep up that positivity.

Do it for yourself and you'll have more space, energy, and time to do the things that bring you joy!

## PUT IT INTO PRACTICE

Compile a list of all the things you have to do in a day. Of course, you probably have your job, but then think about those tiny things you do that take time and energy. These could be doing laundry, making dinner, going grocery shopping, and so on.

.......................................................................................

.......................................................................................

.......................................................................................

.......................................................................................

.......................................................................................

Look at your list, and think about your energy levels. Are you doing too much? Are you feeling strong at the start of each day, or are you drained by the amount of work you have to do?

Get out a new piece of paper and write down some ideas of how you can save yourself time.

- Can you order groceries online?
- Can you send laundry out?
- Can you delegate a task at work?
- Can you put a time limit on your work outside of the workplace?
- Can you get some help with childcare?

If you spend a little time weighing your options, you will be able to find some really wonderful ways to save yourself some time and energy. We have been taught to really prioritize work and forget about rest. It's time to start putting a little bit more focus on that rest.

## CREATIVE EXERCISE

On a separate piece of paper, draw an image of you doing work, whether it's typing an email or doing the laundry. Next to that image, draw a picture of you practicing rest. Sketch yourself reading a book, watching a TV show, or enjoying a glass of wine.

Look at these two pictures and note the idea of balance. You both work and play. One does not take precedence over the other. You need both for a happy, supported life.

# Conclusion

Some people come alive when they work because they get to showcase their skills or delve into something they really love. But even if you love your job, you can still get burnt out. Start squeezing in more rest, and look for unique ways to save yourself energy and time!

# Chapter Twelve

## Look at How You Love

> "
> You have been criticizing yourself for years and it hasn't worked. Try approving yourself and see what happens.
> —*Louise Hay*
> "

Love makes the world go round. Who we love and how we love say so much about us. The people we love, be they friends, partners, or family members, become a part of us because we love them. Our relationships guide how we live our lives, but sometimes we get too focused on external things like work or stress, that we forget how to love and love well. Within that same rush, we can forget how to love ourselves well too.

We do things and say things to ourselves we would never say to another person, especially not someone we love! The point of life is to enjoy it and savor all the beautiful experiences contained within it. But we can become our own harshest critics as we find ourselves not measuring up. Maybe we have yet to achieve the career goal of our dreams. Our physical appearance might leave us frustrated. On top of all that, it's easy to sit around wishing we'd made different choices and become a completely different person when we should honor ourselves.

As you work towards switching your thought patterns toward the positive and adjusting your outlook, you need to look at how you love. By reflecting on this, you can better understand how you can start to adjust the way you love yourself.

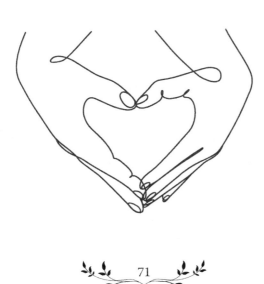

## PUT IT INTO PRACTICE

Look at your relationships, both past, and present. Ask yourself:

- What kind of a partner was I?

  ...................................................................................................

  ...................................................................................................

- How did I love that other person?

  ...................................................................................................

  ...................................................................................................

- What positive things might that person say about me that I wouldn't say about myself?

  ...................................................................................................

  ...................................................................................................

After you've taken some time with this, write down some ideas of how you could turn that ability to love others with kindness, compassion, and understanding onto yourself.

Take it a step further, and thinking about all relationships whether romantic or platonic, write down 100 things you bring to the table. This could be tough at first, but you'll get into it. Examples of this could be how you're quick to compliment, or you enjoy making people laugh. The simplest thing can go a long way. Get these traits down on the list.

Spend some time looking at this list and just remember how wonderful you are. Remember how many unique qualities you bring to the world and to relationships with others. Instead of focusing only on your flaws or how you don't feel you measure up, think about all your strengths. Love yourself in the way you deserve.

## CREATIVE EXERCISE

Next to the 100 items on this list, try to think of unique ways you can show love with this skill. It will take time to get through all 100, so take it step by step. If you're generous, expressive, or a great listener, imagine how you might extend that quality in a new way that makes you feel loved while you extend love to others.

# Conclusion

We learn how to love others way before we learn how to love ourselves. But we are just as important, and we also deserve love from within ourselves. The more you love yourself, the more it will come shining out of you, bringing wonderful energy to the world.

# Part Four: Love Your Perseverance

# Chapter Thirteen

## Tell Your Story

> So long as the memory of certain beloved friends live in my heart, I shall say that life is good.
> —*Helen Keller*

One of the wonderful parts about being you is that you are wholly unique. We are all unique, and we each have our own story to tell. Sometimes, it can feel like we get totally drowned out by the number of people in the world over time. It's easy to fall into the pit of, how could I possibly matter?

And yet, you matter more than you could possibly know. The world needs you to stay true to yourself so that it can continue turning. You may doubt if you're

story is worth telling, but the story of you is precious. When we share our story, we are sharing who we are, and how we've joined into the fabric of life.

Everyone deserves to tell their story, and you can too, in any way you wish to do it.

## PUT IT INTO PRACTICE

Telling your story looks different for each person. If you aren't normally someone who likes to share very often because it makes you feel vulnerable or uncomfortable, consider trying to tell more of your story to others. It could start with your partner, then challenge yourself to share more with friends and family. A therapy session can be a great place to start. Perhaps you don't like the story you have for whatever reason. You might feel ashamed about things in your past or have trauma you would rather keep hidden. It will take time, but start taking ownership of the story you have. There is no longer any need to hide or keep running away from who you are. Start sharing, and you will feel yourself beginning to open up and feel set free.

Stop being afraid or ashamed of the journey you have to share. Own it. Enjoy it. That story is all your own.

## CREATIVE EXERCISE

Create a scrapbook of your personal history. If you like doing crafts, then you can head to your local craft store to get all the supplies you need. Devote at least one page to each major event in your life that changed you.

Collect items that meant something to you, like your first movie ticket stub, or a program from a live music event. These are all part of who you are and the story you've created in your life.

# Conclusion

Too much time is wasted on feeling ashamed or hiding away from our story. Your story is who you are. It's what makes you the beautiful you that you are. Start telling your story and setting yourself free!

# Chapter Fourteen

## Be Your Own Guide to Your Dreams

> " Find out who you are and
> do it on purpose.
> —*Dolly Parton* "

Aspiration makes us human. That drive to do more gives us hope for whatever lies just ahead of us. All we need to do is take the first step. But in a society of groundedness and concrete actions and beliefs, it can be tough to have dreams. We are taught to always be practical, thinking of money, security, or family.

However, it can be incredibly freeing to just let yourself dream. Dream big, dream high, and think about all the things you would love to accomplish in

your life. Do you want to be a writer? Do you want to own your own business? Do you want to record your own album? Hang onto that vision of yourself. It can be as big or small as you like, but allow yourself that freedom to dream.

This freedom often gets stifled without a plan, but it's always possible to transform a dream into a goal.

## PUT IT INTO PRACTICE

We need to give our dreams relevance. The things we imagine are important and deserve our attention. Once we start taking action towards a dream; it becomes a goal. Grab your journal or a piece of paper and start writing down five things you want to accomplish in your life.

Give yourself a number of years in which you wish to accomplish these things. Ideas include:

- You want to work towards a promotion at your job
- You want to relocate to a completely new town
- You want to write a book about your life.

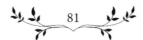

On the next page, write down the steps you can take to progress toward that dream. It has now turned into a goal. Now, you aren't just dreaming. You're giving credence to your dreams and making them a reality.

## CREATIVE EXERCISE

Think about what your life will look like once you've achieved one of your goals. Envision it, and draw it out. This can be an image of you, an achievement, or a scene in your future life when you accomplish your goal.

# Conclusion

Dreams bring us together as women and keep us united. Your imagination brings out your more authentic self. It helps you delve into yourself and discover your true passions. Take this time to get into that process and discover something new about yourself.

# Chapter Fifteen

## Spark Your Creativity

> "Make the most of yourself by fanning the tiny, inner sparks of possibility into flames of achievement.
> —*Golda Meir*

Your perseverance and ability to move through the difficult times in your life is a gift. One way to keep yourself going is to spark your creativity. People think that without the official title of artist, they can't draw or paint, or that they have no creativity.

But creativity is within everyone's grasp. It likes to take on a new shape in each person's hands, but that doesn't make anyone more or less able to create. No matter what you do to express yourself; write, sculpt, dance, anything - your inner artist is your own.

I want to challenge you to love this side of yourself and give it the time it deserves. Take some time every week to do something creative that's focused all on you. Time to make room for personal expression.

## PUT IT INTO PRACTICE

What do you love to do? What sparks your imagination and really takes you out of reality and gets your creative juices flowing?

- Do you love to watercolor?

  ..............................................................................................

  ..............................................................................................

- Do you love interior design?

  ..............................................................................................

  ..............................................................................................

- Do you love flower arranging?

  ..............................................................................................

  ..............................................................................................

- Do you love crafting and building?

........................................................................................

........................................................................................

- Do you love composing music?

........................................................................................

........................................................................................

Don't do this for money or gain; creativity isn't about that. Carve out some time each week to do something creative just for creativity's sake. For example, if you love photography, set out once a week in your city and take pictures of places you love.

Doing something creative will boost your happiness, your overall well-being, and help you persevere during those more difficult times.

## CREATIVE EXERCISE

Think about your three biggest passions in your life. On three separate pieces of paper, draw each of them or an image that represents them. What colors and shapes are your passions? How do you envision them? How can you tap into them in your life?

# Conclusion

Creativity gets left on the sidelines of our lives too often. We forget that it's part of who we are, and when we spend time doing something creative, we are actually giving our brains a chance to get some respite from the daily grind. Get sparking!

# Chapter Sixteen

## Optimize Your System

> " Loving yourself isn't vanity. It's sanity.
> —*Katrina Mayer* "

Just like technology, sometimes we can all use an update. When we get busy, we get so focused on the tasks at hand that we open ourselves up to mental or physical wear and tear. It's only natural, but sometimes we're using a system that's just a bit outdated. It's not serving us any longer, and it's time to change it.

When we optimize our systems, we are finding ways to save energy, time, and resources to get the most out of our lives. Something that's worked really well for you in the past might not be working so well anymore.

For example, maybe getting up and exercising in the morning worked great for you when you were younger or before you had your children. But now, you're a bit busy in the morning making sure the kids get off to school all right. However, you might not realize right away that your system needs a change.

When your old flow doesn't cut it, it's time for a reset. So you can't run in the mornings. Maybe go for a run just after work before the kids get home from school. Or consider working out after they've gone to bed.

Everyone's different, but it's time to start taking stock of your system and see if you don't need an entire system overhaul to get you going again.

## Put It into Practice

What systems do you already have in place in your life? Think about work, home life, health, sleep, and more. As you reflect on each of them, think about what's working for you really well and what seems to escape you.

Have you made progress in these areas? Or are there some places where you're lagging? Start thinking about new systems you could put in place or just systems you could update. These could be changes to your sleep schedule, exercise routine, order of work during the workday, and so much more.

## Creative Exercise

Select an abstract image to color. As you color, think about your life as full of different systems all working together.

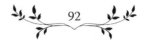

# Conclusion

We can all use an update every now and again. Even if something worked for us in the past, it doesn't mean the same old system will work on the new and improved you. Do a quick scan, and see where your life could use a bit of polishing up!

# Part Five:
# Love Yourself,
# Period

# Chapter Seventeen

## Show Yourself Gratitude

> **"** Whatever you appreciate and give thanks for will increase in your life.
>
> —*Sanaya Roman* **"**

The practice of gratitude is proven to make people happier, healthier, and live a life of meaning. When we focus on giving thanks for the good things we see in life, we notice more incredible things every day. Positive events start coming to the forefront of our minds, and gratitude emerges with less and less effort.

While it can often be easier to say thank you to others, it can be very difficult to say thanks to yourself. This is a chance for you to focus on giving yourself a

word of thanks when you accomplish something. It could be something small such as being patient in a stressful situation, or it could be something bigger, like starting your own business.

Say thanks to yourself more often, and you will turn yourself from being the enemy or a stumbling block to your happiness, into a friend.

## PUT IT INTO PRACTICE

Keep a stack of thank you cards always at the ready. Colorful sticky notes work as well. Keep them with you at the office, at home, and in your purse. Use them when you do something that works towards your health, your dreams, or your overall well-being.

Say thank you to yourself when you exercise all the days you wanted to that week, when you cook a nutritious and delicious meal, or when you set a healthy boundary with someone or something. There are so many things to look for in your life and so many things to thank yourself for.

## CREATIVE EXERCISE

Sketch a symbol of gratitude that makes you think of appreciation whenever you look at it. It can help you remember to be thankful for yourself. This could be an image of a sun, a flower you love, a mandala, whatever you want to help you turn your mind towards saying thanks!

# Conclusion

There is so much you do in your life. Don't wait for others to say thank you. Say it to yourself, and show gratitude for all you accomplish and work through each and every day.

# Chapter Eighteen

## Count Your Blessings

> "Always remember to smile and look up at what you got in life.
> —*Marilyn Monroe*"

Growing up, did your parents ever tell you to 'count your blessings' instead of just complaining? As a kid, it's hard to do that since the bad things can be all so glaring. But now that you're an adult, this idea of focusing on what you've got instead of what you've not can really turn your life around in so many beautiful ways.

The concept of counting your blessings fits along nicely with the art of practicing gratitude. But while I spoke of showing gratitude to yourself, in this chapter, I challenge you to count your blessings in all areas of your life. What better way to foster positivity and joy in your life if you're always focused on counting up those wonderful blessings of yours?

Blessings come in all shapes and sizes. They can be people, events, objects, successes, and so much more. Don't focus only on one area when you're counting up your blessings. Look at the whole of your life and everything in it. What good things are happening to you? What good things do you already have going on in your life?

## PUT IT INTO PRACTICE

Everyone needs to make time to stop and think about what they've been blessed with in their life. Carve out a little time to sit down and make a list of your blessings. Ask yourself:

- What people can you be thankful for?

......................................................................................................

......................................................................................................

- Who has helped you at work, at home, in the community?

  .................................................................................................................

  .................................................................................................................

- Do you have good health?

  .................................................................................................................

  .................................................................................................................

- Do you have wonderful friends?

  .................................................................................................................

  .................................................................................................................

- Do you have a family who loves and supports you?

  .................................................................................................................

  .................................................................................................................

- Is your partner kind and compassionate?

  .................................................................................................................

  .................................................................................................................

- Are your children healthy and happy?

  ........................................................................................

  ........................................................................................

- Do you have a roof over your head?

  ........................................................................................

  ........................................................................................

- Is there enough money to keep you and your family safe and content?

  ........................................................................................

  ........................................................................................

- Do you enjoy your job?

  ........................................................................................

  ........................................................................................

- Do you love your house and where you live?

  ........................................................................................

  ........................................................................................

There are so many ways to look for blessings, and the more things you can list, the more positive things you can focus on. Now, reflect on the word gratitude. What does this word mean in your life?

Brainstorm how you can show more gratitude in your life and show appreciation for the blessings you've been counting. Maybe you can invite a kind neighbor over for a drink or dinner to show your appreciation for them. Perhaps you can offer your time in some volunteer work to say thank you by giving back. Push yourself to say thank you in a new way and keep your eyes on those blessings.

## CREATIVE EXERCISE

Write out the word gratitude in big bubble letters on a large piece of paper. Inside each bubble letter, draw an image of a blessing you're thankful for. You can also draw in ways to show your gratitude to yourself and to others for those blessings. Post this picture up somewhere to help remind you of all your blessings and how can focus on gratitude.

# Conclusion

It's proven that people who focus on their blessings instead of what they don't have are much happier. Wouldn't you be too if all you focused on was your great family, your incredible job, and/or your good friends? Keep smiling by counting up your blessings. More blessings will come your way. You just have to look for them.

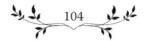

# Chapter Nineteen

---

## Rethink Your Space

> We do not need magic to transform the world. We carry all of the power we need inside of ourselves already.
>
> —*J.K. Rowling*

Home is where the heart is. Everyone wants their home to be a place of safety, love, and warmth. We want a place where people can come and receive love and speak without judgment. Think about your space and the welcome you give to others as well as yourself.

Do you and others feel you can be yourself in your home? Is it a safe space where you can escape from the struggles of the world and just kick back and relax? Start focusing on your space and reflecting on how it

feels for yourself and others. The more wonderfully accepting and welcoming your home is, the better both you, and your family and friends will feel.

## PUT IT INTO PRACTICE

A welcoming home goes beyond opening your doors to your family, friends, and neighbors. It means creating a space that gives you what you need. It should be a sanctuary where they can speak freely and share with you without receiving judgment.

Exemplify this in your home by redecorating your entryway to provide a more positive, open space. Add a wreath; put out potted plants with strings of lights on them; hang up a wreath, or paint your front door a warm, inviting color.

Also, make sure to have a room where people can sit and talk and feel free to enjoy themselves. Anyone and everyone can come to that room. Add a special room for yourself as well. This space is just for you, a safe space where you can just be. This could be a reading nook, a place for yoga or meditation, or a place to journal.

## CREATIVE EXERCISE

Sketch out a visual of a welcoming image for the front of your home. How else can you add decorative and welcoming touches to this part of your house? You can design it in reality or design an image that reminds you to keep that open-door policy going.

# Conclusion

Everyone deserves a space to which they can run to. Your friends, family, and other loved ones deserve this space, and you can create it. But remember to make a space for yourself too.

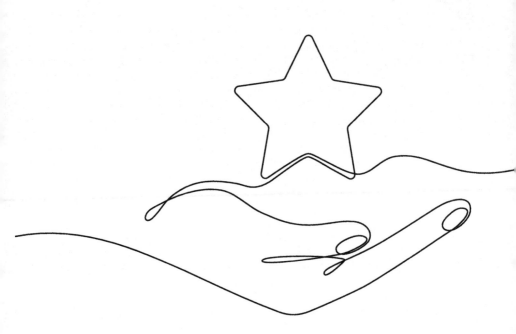

# Chapter Twenty

Hit the Reset Button

 Women need solitude in order to find
again the true essence of themselves.

—*Anne Morrow Lindbergh*

The daily grind is a tiring one. It's not just about the job, but it's all the little aspects of life. Things like laundry, driving kids to practices, helping elderly relatives, and so much more can really tire us out. To show yourself love, start thinking about times when you can pause and give yourself the space to process everything. With all we have to do in our lives, this can seem like an impossible task. But it's essential to your well-being, and it's a great way to show yourself that you love yourself. Part of a happy, positive outlook kind of life is loving yourself. You need to

love yourself so much so that you can give yourself permission to take a bit of a break.

Maybe you already like spending time alone, and you already plug that into your life through reading, exercise, and doing other hobbies on your own that you enjoy. However, my focus in this chapter is to get you to be alone in the quiet.

## PUT IT INTO PRACTICE

Find a way to explore solitude in your life. Look at your calendar and find a day in the near future when you can set aside some time for yourself. Inform others around you that you'll be unavailable this day. Don't allow anyone to change your plan unless it's a true emergency.

Then, find a place where you can enjoy your own company without anyone else getting in the way. No screens, no kids, no distractions. Try for a park or a natural space where you can sit alone and really feel yourself. After you get back home, take a moment to write any reflections about your experience. You will learn to crave this solitude once you begin to make it a practice.

## CREATIVE EXERCISE

Sketch yourself in that solitude space as part of your reflections. What might you notice about yourself in this drawing as compared to the self-portrait you created earlier?

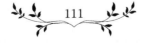

# Conclusion

Sometimes, we just need to turn the volume down. Savoring the silence and learning to love our own company can lead to so much inner peace and confidence. Remember, if you don't love yourself or enjoy your own company, then who will?

# Final Words

Life is hard enough without our negative inner voice getting in the way. It's easy to feel downtrodden when life gets overwhelming, and you feel like you have no one to turn to and nowhere to go. But I encourage you to look to yourself for the strength you need.

Within yourself, you will find a guide, a friend, a confidante, and a voice of encouragement. All you have to do is look for it. Make it a goal to start looking to yourself for guidance as you move through the day-to-day.

Start looking up from your feet and stare confidently ahead of you. Life can get ugly sometimes, but it's also filled with beauty. And if we get too busy hating on ourselves or feeling stressed about things we can't control, then we'll miss out on the wonderful, joyful experiences we can have.

Change your outlook on life to a positive one. Love yourself, love others, and seek out those happy moments.

To bring yourself even more happiness, work on:

- changing your outlook
- celebrating your strengths
- loving your energy
- loving your perseverance
- and loving yourself, period

There is a whole big wonderful life out there for you. But it's up to you to seize it. And all you need is yourself.

# *Bonuses*
## OUR GIFTS FOR YOU

Subscribe to our Newsletter and receive these free materials

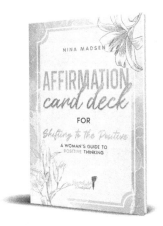

www.specialartbooks.com/free-materials/

# *References*

Instagram: @specialart_books
Facebook Page: Special Art Books
Website: www.specialartbooks.com

# Impressum

For questions, feedback, and suggestions:

support@specialartbooks.com

Nina Madsen, Special Art

Printed in Great Britain
by Amazon

35713003R00066